Merseyside County Museums Occasional Papers 1

Land Tenure in Ince Blundell and Sefton

Ian Bakewell

Merseyside County Council/Merseyside County Museums

Land Tenure in Ince Blundell and Sefton

Ian Bakewell

Merseyside County Museums

ISBN 0 906367 14 X

Artwork by Geoff Phillips
Typing by Susan Brown
Design by Barrie Jones
Printed by Merseyside County Council

British Library Cataloguing in Publication Data

Bakewell, Ian
Land tenure in Ince Blundell.–(Merseyside County Museum's occasional papers; 1)
1.Land tenure–England–Ince Blundell (Merseyside) 2.Ince Blundell (Merseyside) –Antiquities
I.Title II.Series
333.3'23'0942759 HD610.I/

ISBN 0-906367-14-X

Cover illustration:
Peasants paying dues to the lord of the manor from an early 14th century manuscript

Grateful acknowledgements are made to the staff of the Lancashire and Liverpool Record Offices and especial thanks are due to Jen Lewis for additional research and advice in preparing the script.

Contents

Preface

This study is concerned with the medieval and post-medieval land tenure under contrasting types of overlordship in two manors of the parish of Sefton. Ince Blundell was assigned to the Barony of Warrington in the early 12th century and the succeeding barons maintained their superiority at least until the late 16th century though they were never resident in the township. During the medieval period there were a number of free tenants, amongst whom the Blundell family was acknowledged to be in possession of the principal landholding unit. By contrast, Sefton was granted as a military fee to an ancestor of the Molyneux family and, unlike Ince Blundell, was clearly dominated by a single resident lord.

In addition to providing information regarding tenurial relationships and land management the study provides a framework within which it may be possible to assess potential archaeological sites in terms of their tenurial status. It is an area of research which may be usefully extended to other manors for which there is a similar archive of documentary material.

The research for this project was funded by the Manpower Services Commission in 1981 as part of the work of the Archaeological Survey of Merseyside. The Survey was established in 1977 to collect and record archaeological and historical evidence in the County for the period up to 1750. Its work has been supported by the Department of the Environment (Ancient Monuments), Merseyside County Council, the University of Liverpool and the Merseyside Archaeological Society with special funding from the Manpower Services Commission.

Richard Foster
Director of Museums

1.0 Introduction

No established set of criteria exists to define and describe medieval and post-medieval regional landownership; essentially, any examination of landownership poses the question as to what factors decided how the land was originally divided. Without an attempt at seeking such origins, an investigation of the evolution of landholdings in south west Lancashire becomes confused and unsystematic. The use and division of the land resources can be governed by a number of elements : geographical characteristics, patterns of settlement, socio-political arrangements and historical considerations. The classical image of the bilateral manor is invariably hard to discern and 'the ideal type of medieval vill is of course an historical abstraction' (Postan 1972, 111).

The lack of pre-conquest archaeological information regarding south west Lancashire reflects geographical isolation. It was indeed 'a *cul-de-sac* from the strategic point of view' (Walker 1939, 16). The separateness of the area was re-emphasised after 1066; the only fundamental change was one of overlord. The handing over of the region *en masse* was probably as much due to its geographical marginality as any other consideration. Nevertheless, the great potential wealth of south west Lancashire in the arable economy of the medieval period found its very roots in these isolated geographical characteristics. 'South west Lancashire by virtue of its lower altitude, has higher average temperatures and a lower rainfall and, in addition, it lies in the "shadow" of the highland mass of Wales which reduces the effect of the prevailing south westerly winds and gives rise to far more favourable climatic conditions than south east Lancashire' (Walker 1939, 35). In the middle ages arable farming was widespread, assarting commonplace and agricultural prosperity expanding.

The relationship between geographical features and settlement patterns is axiomatic. With regard to place names, British elements survive in topographic features (Alt, Ince) but English influence can be associated with settlement (Melling, Lydiate, Thornton). Moreover, Scandinavian influence in coastal regions equates well with their mode of approach, and an admixture of celtic and Norse (e.g. Grimsargh, Lancashire) reveals the Irish origins of the settlers. The presence of inhabitants of different ethnic backgrounds led to an amalgam of celtic, Anglian and Scandinavian customs which left their mark on social arrangements. It is perhaps at this juncture that in historical terms, an assessment of landownership becomes important. In order to survive, any society must order its relationships upon the dictates of economic production: it has to use and develop available technology and accomodate demographic change. In the case of this examination the relative strength or absence of feudal elements in landownership was under examination.

Evidence of open field agriculture may be sought both on the ground and by means of documentary material. This system of farming was 'the means by which land was cultivated by the inhabitants of a township, who worked their holdings in unenclosed parcels' (Taylor 1981, 13). Such a simplistic definition disguises the complexity of land management. How does such an arrangement arise? How is it administered? At the outset, open field agriculture demanded certain communal activities although how these activities were organised is itself a matter of contention. The essential problem of field subdivision has prompted two basic interpretations. Seebohm contended that subdivided fields arose out of joint ploughing requirements - the joining together to form an ox team (Dodgshon 1981, 130-37). The theory revolves around the concept of the fundemental land unit being one strip or selion that formed a single day's measure of work. In essence, this implies that technical determinism led to the formation of the strip field system. Vinogradoff's alternative hypothesis was founded upon the idea that bovates and virgates denoted the division of land in a township and that because the quality of the land was variable it had to be subdivided to ensure equal shares. Thus in broadest terms the reasons for the development of open field agriculture can be reduced to two alternatives - that of piecemeal colonisation or pre-determined shareholding based on communal tenure.

How the system was administered is not immediately clear; ‘the mantle of communalism, which regular layouts and open field husbandaries testify to, may have been donned later out of choice (or lordly coercion) when the opportunity arose to re-organise or rationalise the system’ (Dodgshon 1981, 143). Medieval England possessed multifarious commonfield systems whose forms were governed by six main features: the ownership of the waste, the patterns of field and holding layout, methods of fallow grazing, regulation of cropping and the mode of regulation. Evidence relating to the executive responsibilities of operating an open field system has been researched (Vinogradoff 1892). Indeed, there have been attempts to penetrate the static tableau feudal relationships and it has been forcibly suggested that, where a township fell under the control of a plurality of lordships, the only effective administrative body would have been the medieval vill. Paradoxically, this may not have led to a highly developed communalised land system. It has been argued that, under feudalism, the relative shortage of labour meant that an efficient use of the same was required and that the imposition of a regular commonfield system had this effect (Campbell 1981, 127). If the rationalisation of commonfield agriculture was a function of the growth of feudal order, it follows that it would have progressed furthest where there was a tradition of strong and undivided lordship and where there existed a high proportion of customary tenants. Medieval tenurial arrangements did not exist in a vacuum. The fact that the common and town fields fell under the primary ownership of manors, and that manorial grants devolved specified communal rights, gives some clue as to how the reality of ‘shareholding’ in the open fields fitted into a stricter tenurial framework. It is true that in the 17th and 18th centuries the tenants and freeholders of Sefton Parish divided duties on a communal basis within a manorial court. Nevertheless, it is equally indisputable that the court belonged to the lord and was governed by his exactions and lease relationships.

The arrangements between landholders were obviously affected by other extraneous factors. Demographic change was not an unimportant element. As population increased, the division of landholdings would probably have progressed despite the absence of any legal tradition of partible inheritance. Similarly, a change in management techniques, notably a general drift from demesne farming to rents, would result in change and re-organisation of landownership. Direct management of demesnes was practical when society was relatively stable and lords could control local officials; such conditions appear to have prevailed at certain periods in the 13th century. On the other hand, direct management was more difficult and less profitable when general conditions worsened, this being apparent in the mid-decades of the 12th century and in the second half of the 14th and the greater part of the 15th centuries.

Undoubtedly, the most distinct feature of landholding in the post-medieval era was the emergence of enclosure. It would appear that it had no traumatic effects in south west Lancashire and that voluntary enclosure had prodeeded throughout the medieval period. The implication that open field agriculture was being rationlised alongside the closes and closures specified in land documents serves to reiterate the question as to how the soil was originally allocated.

2.0 The Documents

The documents employed in this investigation can best be divided into two general headings; primary and secondary sources. The primary sources have in the main consisted of private family muniments and 19th century tithe awards. The secondary sources are more miscellaneous encompassing both local and national records.

The most comprehensive documents of post-medieval landownership are undoubtedly the tithe awards. The combination of the mapped and numbered buildings and fields with the corresponding schedule of ownership, field names, use and acreage allow scope for definite conclusions. However, as a guide to landownership trends they are sterile if taken alone. Being exclusively a product of the modern period, a tithe assessment cannot reflect adequately medieval systems. In the logical framework, they are initially best combined with the 18th century Molyneux land survey (Lancs. RO DDM 14/12). Continuity and extent of holdings can be compared and, in addition, the available estate maps reveal the area of manorial lands. Having established discernable links, rent rolls and leases are helpful in the detailing of land administration and in the medieval period in outlining early agricultural systems. Other elements of importance in this context include the hearth taxes, manorial court rolls and accounts. From this evidence it is possible to construct an overview of the tenurial relationships and the obligations which governed land division.

The secondary source material can be divided into published transcripts and general works which attempt to establish historical continuity. In the former category, such material as the Recusant Rolls, Lancashire Inquests and collections of medieval monastic grants are invaluable. In the latter material, The Victoria County History is perhaps the principal secondary source work and is complemented by other more subjective writings (e.g. Caroe and Gordon 1893). The Recusant Rolls, Papists' Estates and Land Tax Schedules were not referred to directly owing to misgivings expressed by Wilson (1980, 63-92).

The most obvious problem with documents is access and availability. The wealth of material at the Public Record Office and other pertinent sources (e.g. the Dodsworth MSS at the Bodleian, Oxford) could not be examined. Moreover, the material which was available was notably 'patchy' in the medieval period both in terms of content and condition. The secondary works, notably once again the VCH, evoke problems of emphasis. Earlier local historians' obsession with genealogies and the marital fortunes of the gentry did not always unearth the complexity of medieval society. This gives rise to difficulties of interpretation, in particular seeking definitions of the manor, the standing of freeholders and the implications of the evidence of feudal heirarchies. The virtual total absence of maps before the 18th century and the regional variations in land measurement make it almost impossible to construct any long term outlines of specific landownership. Most of the plausible inferences have to come from field names and passing reference to arrangements within those fields (e.g. selions, butts). Unfortunately, the documents often prompt more questions than they answer.

3.0 Ince Blundell (fig. 1)

3.1 Medieval

The origins and determinents of landownership in Ince Blundell were obviously guided by geographical considerations. At the turn of this century it was recorded that the township 'embraces a considerable area of flat fen country laid out in pastures and cultivated fields where corn, root crops and clover hay are produced in rich alluvial soil' (VCH 3, 1907, 78). The name Ince may denote an island and probably refers to a small piece of high ground in the midst of a marsh (Ekwall 1922, 118).

Little evidence can be gleaned about settlement before 1066 although later field names do imply an admixture of different ethnic influences. Rowenholm and Carceld of medieval Ince contain elements of Old Norse whilst Ekwall (1922, 176) has suggested that the Lohangile and Loxangile (Lancs. RO DDIn 53/2 & 10 respectively) are possibly equatable with the Old English 'angel' developing senses such as 'bend of a river'. The first definite pointer to medieval landownership in Ince Blundell comes with the compilation of Domesday. In 1066, Hinne was held by three thegns for three manors. It was assessed at half a hide and worth above the customary rent of eight shillings. There are a number of important elements to be recognised in this short entry from the Norman survey. Firstly, the willingness of Anglo-Norman society to embrace Anglo-Saxon legislative conventions as expressed in the usage of thegn and hide. Furthermore, in terms of measurement, it has been suggested that in the regional context, one hide represented six ploughlands or carucates and thus 11th century Ince was regarded as possessing three ploughlands or twenty-four oxgangs. Topographically, an oxgang could include anything between 7 and 50 acres depending on the quality of the land. Clearly, to attempt to delineate the boundaries of the vill at this historical moment would be wholly conjectural. What is certain is the interrelationship Domesday Book reveals between feudal military obligation and landownership (thegn is an essentially militaristic term with its origins in Old English) and, as is common with earlier medieval history, only the 'manorial' aspect of landholding is visible in the township at this stage. However, it would be incorrect to presume that the three manors of Domesday actually denote the presence of three demesnes. One or more of the manorial units were probably the extrinsic holdings of other settlements and must be considered as such.

3.1.1 *Landownership*

In the early 12th century, Ince was included in the Barony of Warrington and was given by Pain de Vilers to Roger de Stainsby together with half a ploughland in Barton (Lancashire). Superior lordship remained with Warrington and this feudal hierarchical structure remained intact into the post-medieval period as is witnessed by Robert Blundell securing commutation of knight's service to free socage for the manor in 1596-97, paying one penny per annum as acknowledgement and doing fealty to the chief lordship of Warrington (VCH 3, 1907, 82). With the death of Roger de Stainsby the manor reverted to the Barony of whom it was subsequently held by Richard Blundell. In 1212 the Testa de Nevill recorded '...*Idem Paganus dedit Rogero de Stainesbi Ines, scilicet iij carucatas terre, et preter hoc iiij bovatas terre in Barton, quam Willelmus Blundel tenet de Willelmo Pincerna per servicium militare unde x carucate faciunt feudum j militis*' (Book of Fees 1921, 207) (The same Pain gave Ines, that is three carucates of land, to Roger de Stainesbi, and besides this four bovates of land in Barton, which William Blundel holds of William le Boteler by knight's service, where ten carucates make the fee of one knight (Farrer ed. 1903, 7)). It seems that the principle of primogeniture was well established by this time with Richard Blundell having granted his complete holding to his son who was enfeoffed for knight's service for 3½ ploughlands where ten constituted a fee. The return for 1242-43 indicates that, for administrative purposes at least, the assessment of the vill may not have altered for nearly two hundred years 'Richard Blundell holds the third part of a knight in Hynis (Ince) and Barton of the said fee' (Farrer ed. 1903, 147). The implications of this evidence will be returned to later. In provincial terms, it would appear that, from the late 12th century onwards, the Blundell family was acknowledged as being in possession of the chief landholding unit. In a number of documents Blundells are referred to as 'Lord of Ines' (Lancs. RO DDIn 53/13 & 25 and DDBl 44/2). Sir William Blundell was the first named of twelve knights chosen to perambulate Lancashire's forests, a commission occasioned by an Act of 9 Henry III 1225, decreeing that all forests made by Henry II, Richard and John should be disforested (Gibson 1876, 88-89). In the latter half of the 14th century, the suffix Blundell was attached to Ince and has remained to this day. An Inquisition at the death of William Blundell in 1547 revealed that he 'was seized in his Demesne of Free of and in four messuages, 100 Acres of Land, 300 Acres of Meadow, 100 Acres of Pasture and 80 Acres of Heath with ye appurtenances in Ince Blundell' (Lancs. RO DDIn 64/58). Nevertheless, the medieval development of landownership in Ince was not totally dominated by the Blundells. Despite their preponderant influence the township did not constitute the medieval ideal of the manor/vill relationship.

Figure 1 Location of Ince Blundell and Sefton

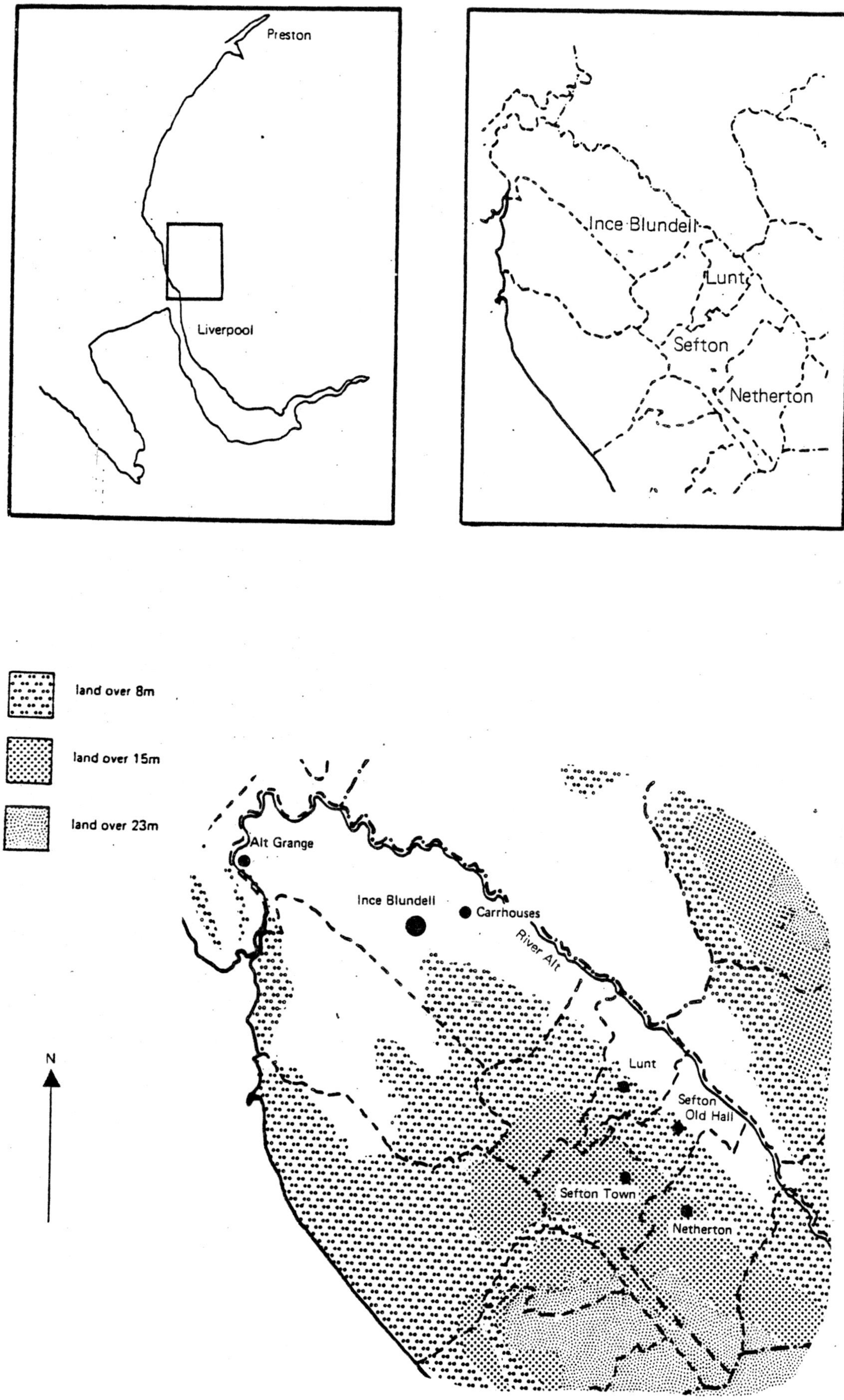

An important element throughout the medieval centuries was the establishment of the Cistercian presence in the area now known as Alt Grange, situated to the north of the present village. It has been noted that, 'In the medieval period, the monasteries, above all the Cistercian houses from the early 12th century onwards, were responsible for many changes in the landscape' (Hoskins 1955, 101). The Blundell 'gifts' to the grange must not be underestimated in the early medieval epoch. In the early 13th century William Blundell gave the Monks of Stanlaw his mill upon the Alt and his land called Scholes. His son, Richard, added half the land of Alt Marsh which Robert, citizen of York, had drained by dykes (VCH 3, 1907, 79). In the same century William Blundell became a benefactor bestowing a piece of meadow in Ince Marsh and foregoing milling rights in favour of the monks of Alt (Morton 1928, unpub. no.12). The concession of milling rights, a central feature of any feudal economy, is a significant confirmation of the local importance of the Grange. The monastic holding at Ince *was* being extended in the 12th and 13th centuries and despite its extreme marginality, probably pre-dates the piecemeal assarting nearer the village itself. Between 1347 and 1351 the abbot prosecuted William Blundell of Ince and others for money owing and in 1441 Henry Blundell took action against John, Abbot of Whalley, for supposed non-repair of a ditch which caused flood damage in Ince and Little Crosby (VCH 3, 1907, 83).

Following the suppression of Whalley Abbey at the Dissolution in 1537, Alt Grange was purchased by Richard Molyneux. This was not the Molyneuxes' first appearance in the township. Around 1260, William of Molineux granted to Richard Flok 'a messuage in Ynes ...in the marsh, rendering yearly 7d.' (Lancs. RO DDIn 53/5). In 1479 Thomas Molyneux of Sefton and William, son of Robert Blundell, reached agreement that the former should not enclose any part of Ince Marsh until the death of William Blundell, father of Robert (VCH 3, 1907, 81). An inquisition following the death of Sir William Molyneux in 1548 indicated that he held 4 messuages, 40 acres of land, 4 acres of meadow, 20 acres of pasture, 2 acres of wood, 10 acres of heath, moss and turbary in Ince Blundell held by socage of the heirs of James Blundell esq. at 2s. 9d. rent (Lancs. RO DDIn 53/78).

The essential feature emphasised by the monastic holding and Molyneux presence is that Ince Blundell was not dominated by a monolithic demesne. This characteristic is underlined by an examination of the social strata below the aristocracy. Although the servile status of villeins can be glimpsed in certain 13th century documents, such as when William Blundell granted to William Blundell *juvenis* four oxgangs of land in Ince with the three villeins who occupied them (VCH 3, 1907, 79), this particular township appears to have possessed a strong tradition of free tenants. In 1283, eleven free tenants were recorded; in 1332 there were seven contributors to the Exchequer Lay Subsidy and in a 1344 deed, ten freeholders and ten leaseholders under the manor were cited (Gibson 1876, 96-7). In terms of population assessment, the Exchequer Subsidy may not have any true reflection on the size of the township. The tax was only levied upon those whose possessions were valued above ten shillings and it was managed by local residents. It can be surmised from this that for both honest and fraudulent reasons, a number of people did not contribute. More important, however, were the relative sums that those who had to meet the fifteenth tax actually paid. Two people, Jordan de Morhouses and Robert Ballardson, gave 3s. 4d. and 3s. 8d. respectively whilst William Blundell's payment was 3s. 0d. Robert Flock also paid 3s. 0d. which effectively means that of those listed, only 50% of the residents contributed *less* than William Blundell, 'Lord of Ynes'. Ecomonically and perhaps in terms of land management, although this cannot be assessed, it appears that medieval Ince contained a strong under-tenancy. Whether this was a remnant of pre-conquest land ownership or a later evolutionary process is difficult to decide. The position in 1344 with ten free tenants and a similar number of leaseholders is of interest because of the latter group. This was the era of demesne high farming and extensive direct management. However, it appears that in Ince, the drift towards rents had already begun and may have been well established.

Figure 2 Ince Blundell 1844

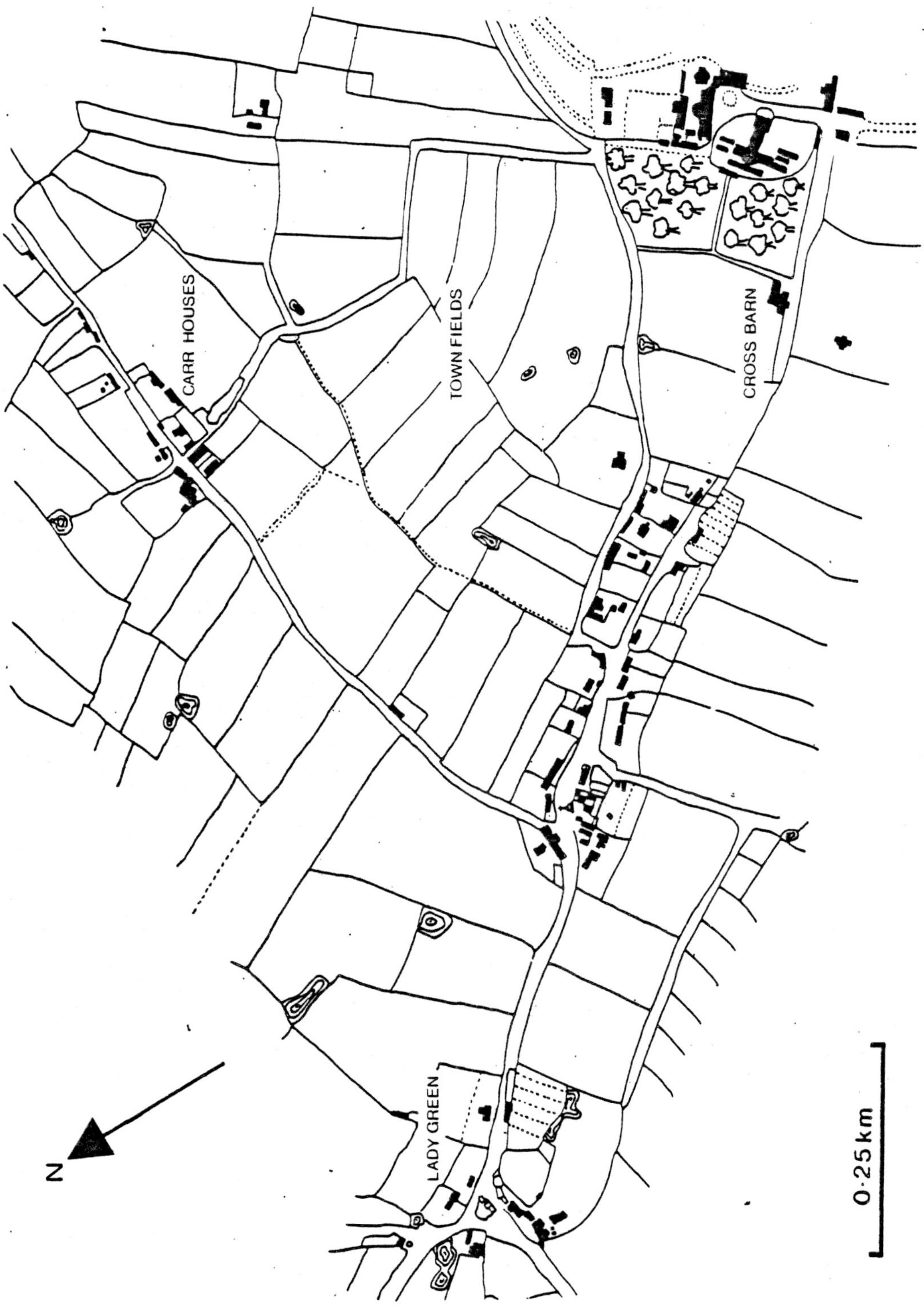

The Poll Tax Returns 1377-1381 reveal that thirty people were taxed in the vill of Ince Blundell (PRO E1179/130/29). Although these lists are valuable for tracing the principal landowning families, they must not be relied upon as a sure basis for demographic calculations. This national subsidy in particular was notorious for the successful evasion it provoked. The documentary indicators which reveal the medieval undertenantry emphasise the importance of the Ballard and Blanchard families. Both may have preceded the post-conquest aristocracy and may have possessed substantial holdings and influence. It has been suggested that one ploughland (i.e. 1/3 of the town's arable) held by Robert, the brother of John Blundell, in the first half of the 13th century, came into the hands of the Ballard family (VCH 3, 1907, 80). In 1351 Emma, widow of Robert Ballard, and her son Thomas and others brought a plea of novel disseisin against William Blundell touching tenements in Ince and in 1355 14 acres were claimed in Ince by Thomas Ballard and Margery his wife from William Blundell and Joan, his wife (VCH 3, 1907, 83 n3). Just over one hundred years later in 1463, there was a contest between William Blundell and Richard Ballard concerning the division of the waste. The latter's supporters occupied the disputed land and removed the Blundell's cattle which they found there. Although arbitration prevailed in favour of the lord of the manor, the free tenant continued to offer resistance (Gibson 1876, 100).

After a further legal dispute with the Blundells, Robert Ballard secured a right to a third of the waste in 1505 and in 1509 sold a moiety of the ground to William Molyneux of Sefton (Lancs. RO DDIn 53/66c and VCH 3, 1907, 83 n4 respectively). The Ballard action of 1505 was eventually a claim to one third of the manor and *may*, via the ploughland gained in the 13th century, represent a link with the township description of Domesday. This clouds, somewhat, the legalistic norms of superiority as presumed in the Blundell muniments. As Vinogradoff remarked, 'the lord may not over-burden the common and sometimes freeholders try their hand at litigation on the grounds that he sends his cattle to some place where they ought not to go' (Vinogradoff 1892, 272). Evidently, a freeholder would only challenge the 'terre lord' of the vill if he considered that opportunities existed to succeed.

Of the other prominent family, Gilbert Blanchard was in the list of free tenants for 1283, Richard Blanchard paid to the lay subsidy of 1332, Robert son of Richard Blanchard was one of the free tenants of 1344 and Robert and Adam Blanchard contributed to the poll tax of 1381. Between 1249 and 1266 Richard Blundell granted to William, son of Swain Blanchard, two fields in his vill of Ince, at 12d. rent (VCH 3, 1907, 84 n13). Some six hundred years later, two Blanchards were recorded in the tithe apportionment of 1844 although the Ballard family seems to have disappeared during the 16th century, probably due to extinction of the male line (see below p.10). A crude genealogy of the Ballard family is extant but is undated and contains no clear chronology (Lancs. RO DDM 11/17). Despite the dictates of the feudal social order, the evidence does suggest that the Ballards and Blanchards were the living representatives of what amounted to substantial free holdings. In addition, other tenants like the Flocks must have amassed relatively large areas of land and reaped the economic and social benefits accordingly (Lancs. RO DDIn 53/5; Morton 1881, 265-267).

Having glimpsed the central trends in medieval landownership in the vill, it is important to relate these to the structure of land management. Any examination of medieval land organisation should begin with the 'historical abstraction': the demesne and dependent vill. As has been shown, Ince was probably not dominated in its entirety by the Blundells although this observation does not preclude the exercise of feudal rights. Undoubtedly, the Blundells were 'terre lords' (i.e. lords who actually occupied the land) from an early date. The first definitive evidence of this may be seen in a grant of 1366 whereby John de Kenyon, chaplain, gave to Joan, widow of William Blundell, the Manor of Ince, with houses, gardens, orchards, the holt adjoining the said manor, turbary, etc. (Morton and Gibson 1880, 194-96). However, acknowledgement of feudal rights and services prior to this date is not wanting. In an undated grant, presumed to be 13th century, Richard Blundell gave to Benedict, son of

Simon, land 'To have and to hold to him and his heirs of Me and my heirs in hereditary feud' (Morton and Gibson 1880, 190). Also, in an undated agreement already cited between the Abbot of Stanlaw and William, son of John Blundell of Ince, 'William gives *his* Windmill in Ynis with suit of all men: also liberty at *his* Watermill on the river of Alte'. The classic rights of the feudal lord have thus presumably devolved upon the Blundells and it is important to remember that this situation will have permeated all other aspects of exchange and organisation.

3.1.2 *Common Field Agriculture*

Evidence of a common field system in Ince is reasonably plentiful for the medieval period. As with the presence of the free tenantry, it is difficult to assess whether the common practices in Ince pre-empted or evolved within the medieval epoch. Common land was a characteristic in the township soon after 1066. In the early part of the 13th century, William Blundell granted land to the monks of Stanlaw 'with common of pasture of the whole vill of Ince for their sheep and cows, and rights of turbary and housebote' (VCH 3, 1907, 79 n11). In an exchange of 1240-1 with the same monks, Richard Blundell agreed to leave the residue of the marsh between Ince and Scholes untilled for ever as common pasture (VCH 3, 1907, 79 n15). References to 'common pasture' in the documents are of early origin and presumably reflect communal practices of wider extent (Lancs. RO DDIn 53/2 & 10).

With regard to arable farming, the medieval material contains much terminology indicative of townfield systems. In 1332 William Blundell of Ince effected an exchange of property with Agnes his mother in which, amongst other lands, Agnes gave 'a selion lying under the old orchard...a land...one head of which abutts on Morgate...also a land in Carcald called the Cutteslond' (Lancs. RO DDIn 53/27). This is clearly the vocabulary of strip farming and emphasises the importance of open field agriculture. More illuminating was a grant dated 1402 whereby John of the Wodes, chaplain *et al*, gave extensive lands to John Blundell (Lancs. RO DDIn 53/55) (Appendix 1). It is a catalogue of selions dispersed throughout numerous open fields often tenanted by others under the lordship of the Blundells. Identification of the fields was made by relating their position to other features; '...1 place of land called the Marledhey next the Peyselandes' but absolute identification on the ground is sometimes possible only by association with other documentary or landscape evidence.

From the survey of Ince Blundell Townfield, compiled by John Eyes in 1728-29 it is possible to extricate certain names contained in the 1402 grant; Wrangelands, Gapelands and the 'field of Richard Blanchard' which were constituents of the arable townfield (Lancs. RO DDIn 53/102; fig. 3). From the 15th century document cited above there would appear to be, in addition, a townfield system based upon the Peyselandes, Goselands, Toftelondes, the Mylnehill and the Marledearth. On the tithe map of 1844, the field names of the lands which are perched on the eastern edge of the park reiterate the elements of the Peasland, Gosseland hey and Mill hey (Lancs. RO DRL 1/40). The Green Hey in this area also suggests common lands which presumably stretched into the modern environs of the park in the medieval period, (Lancs. RO DDIn dep. 1962, three 18th century maps). An attempt can also be made to locate the Carcald of the 14th and 15th centuries. In strict terms, Carcald probably derives from the Old Norse elements 'kelda' and implies a brushwood area where there is a well or spring (Ekwall 1922, 9). Moreover, it does not appear to have been a single field. In 1332 there was 'a land in Carcald called the Cuttesland' (Lancs. RO DDIn 53/27) and in 1454 an exchange included 'one more (butt) in the more hey of the Carkeld' (Lancs. RO DDIn 53/61a). Although the description of 'land' may be synonymous and interchangeable with the notion of a strip, the extensions upon the central element 'Feathercarkeld', 'Over Carcalt', 'Nether Carcalt' may suggest a large common complex. A tentative equation may be made between the Carkeld and the Geld Hey of the 19th century. The Car element in the name may be descriptive of its position in the area known as Carrhouses rather than a strict reference to any geographical feature.

As regards the expansion of the township and piecemeal enclosure, there is no medieval evidence indicating communal arrangements for clearing and assarting. Nevertheless, as early as the references to common rights, there were contemporary documents showing the practice of enclosure. In an undated grant, William of Molineux gave to Richard Flock a messuage in Ince the width of which was delineated by hedges (Lancs. RO DDIn 53/5). In the second half of the 13th century, William Blundell's gift to the Stanlaw monks was a piece of meadow in Ince Marsh around which Roger de Upton, formerly granger of the Abbey, had made a ditch (VCH 3, 1907, 80 n3). Before 1240, Robert, citizen of York, drained land in Alt Marsh by dykes. Dykes appear to have been used to denote field boundaries and thus, as landmarks, were employed to identify land in exchange (Lancs. RO DDBl 44/2, DDIn 53/13). In an exchange of 1240 between the Abbot of Stanlaw and Richard Blundell, 'the abbot gives the land in the Waste surrounded by the dykes: Richard Blundel gives the marsh between the Mill and the bridge over the Alt at Scippul and the meadow enclosed by William, father of Richard Blundel, lying next the monks meadow' (Lancs. RO DDIn 53/16). It appears that in the marsh and waste areas of the township, enclosed land may have been held in severalty throughout the medieval period and affords a variation to the ideal of communal expansion in open field agriculture. The 1479 agreement regarding Ince Marsh and the Ballard acquisition of one third of the waste imply a control of the land resources by the great landowners but, although they may then have directed communal activities on the land, this is not clear. Indeed, lack of evidence creates a number of paradoxes concerning an interpretation of the vill.

3.1.3 *Township*

The township itself seemed to grow around many classical features: the proximity of the manor to the village, the nucleated settlement, the presence of townfields and the existence of field names such as the Riddings Moss, the Intake and Long Shote all of which imply assarting and extension of the settlement's arable farming. The intricacies of land management are more difficult to ascertain. No manorial court rolls appear to be extant for Ince Blundell and, as late as 1758, there was an agreement between the inhabitants of the township for scouring a watercourse 'made necessary because no manor courts are held' (Lancs. RO DDIn 53/103). This ambiguous statement could mean one of two things; either that manor courts had been held but had ceased or, that the intermixture of the social structure discussed above, militated against a strict feudal system and towards a greater emphasis on informal communal activity. In practice, land administration could have fallen anywhere between these two extremes although the importance of tenurial relationships cannot be overlooked. As a grant of 1332 recorded, 'William, son of William Blundel of Ines, to Robert, son of Gilbert Blanchard of Ines...sufficient turbary in *his* common moss of Ines for one house and hearth, with free carriage way' (Lancs. RO DDBl 44/4).

3.2 Post Medieval

3.2.1 *Landownership*

The 16th century was an important time in Ince for realignment of major landownership. As has already been discussed, the Dissolution of 1537 increased the Molyneux holding within the township. Alt Grange went to a younger branch of the Molyneux family and the estate devolved upon the Seel family through marriage in the 18th century (Lancs. RO DDM 14/12). By the time of the 19th century tithe apportionment, Alt Grange was held from Lord Sefton by an under-tenant, Elizabeth Westhead.

Another crucial transference of land was that of the Ballards to the Molyneuxes. By 1560 the inheritance of Richard Ballard had come to two daughters, Cecily and Dorothy, who had married Richard Thorne and Thomas Massingberd respectively. In 1562 Cecily and Richard Thorne sold their moiety of the third part of the manor of Ince Blundell to Sir Richard Molyneux (VCH 3, 1907, 83 n5). Thomas and Dorothy Massingberd sold their moiety to William Blundell in 1569 which Thomas, the heir of Richard Blundell, then sold to Sir Richard Molyneux, grandson of the above, in 1579 (VCH 3, 1907, 83 n7). This may constitute

Figure 3 Townfields of Ince Blundell 1728-1729

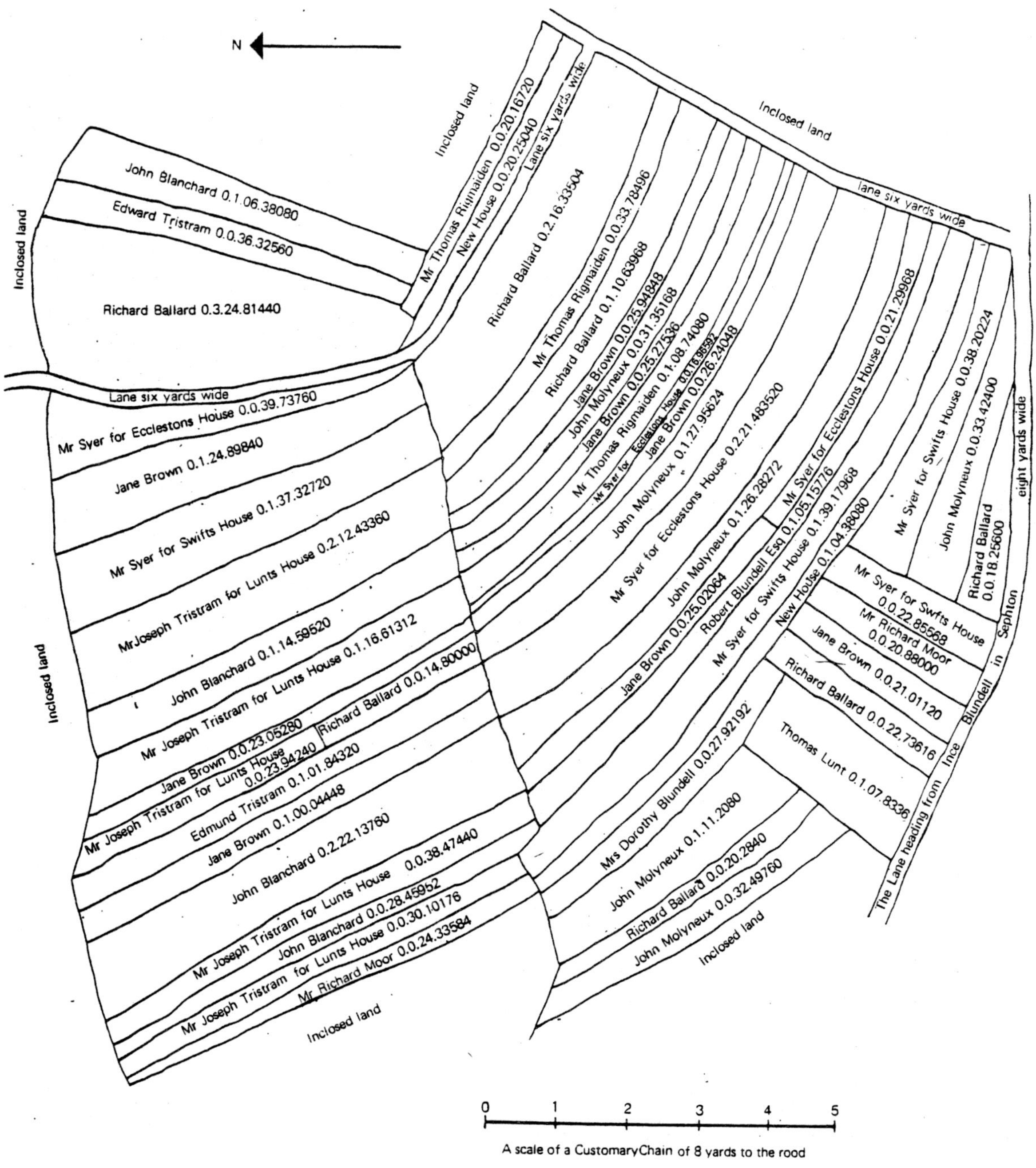

the 'manor of Northend' named in the later Molyneux inquisitions and the holding of 25 customary acres which Richard Bettaugh (*sic*) possessed at North End in 1769 (the holding was known as 'Ballards Tenement').

Overlordship became effectively consolidated from 1500 onwards and, at the same time, the Blundell and Molyneux holdings became increasingly intertwined. As regards the under-tenancy, and the acceptance of leaseholding as the prevalent tenurial relationship. A number of 16th century rentals for Molyneux holdings in Ince survive and one in particular reflects how at the beginning of the post-medieval period Molyneux and Blundell land was interlocked. This document of 1523 itemised rented land in the Black Carre, Syngletons Hey, Eleven Acre and Olde Mersche (Lancs. RO DDM 53/66a). This was possibly land previously in the possession of the Ballards and would account for the Molyneux holding to the east of the township (Lancs. RO DDIn 53/66c). The Blundell holding in Ince remained the most substantial *landbloc* throughout the post-medieval period. In the 1844 tithe apportionment a little over 70% of the township subject to tithe payments was in the ownership of Thomas Weld Blundell (Lancs. RO DRL 1/40). The progression towards this figure had not been a constant growth. An indication of the size of the 16th century demesne can be seen in a marriage settlement of 1550 (Lancs. RO DDIn 64/63). The chief messuage was then designated as 'the halle of Ince...that Close of lande and pasture then called the Gorstie Croft...the holte fyldes...the Cowe heye...the Calff Crofte and the Wodde...the broade heye', land in Ince Field, an acre of land in the Old Marsh, land in the occupation of Thomas Blanchard and James Harrison and a selion of land in Ince Field. The term 'Ince Field' is presumably a generic term covering a field system rather than a physically delineated area.

With the problem of identification, it is not clear either where the 'holte fyldes...the Cowe heye...or the Calff Croft' may have been situated or their extent. Nevertheless, it would appear that in the 16th century, the money values do not reflect a large demesne holding which may have contracted with the spread of rentals. In the following century the Blundell lands were greatly increased at the instigation of Robert Blundell. He purchased the manors of Birkdale, Meandale and Ainsdale in addition to Renacres in Halsall. In the first comprehensive post-medieval account of the manor of Ince Blundell in 1652/53, the lands associated with the hall embraced some 191 acres (acreage size not expressed) excluding the holdings leased to tenants (Lancs. RO DDIn 19/14). In the survey of 1770 the lands of Henry Blundell were expressed in both statutory and customary measures (Lancs. RO DDIn 63/62). By this time, the holdings attached to the capital messuage had reached 258.3.01 statute or 122.0.08 customary acres. In a valuation of 1793 the holding above was 223.0.08 customary acres (Lancs. RO DDIn 68/80). The variance in acreages is perhaps explained by progressive and regressive movements in leaseholding. At the cessation of any particular lease, the principal landowner may have found it economically advantageous to retain the holding and similarly, at other times, to profit by an extension of leases.

3.2.2 *Minor landowners and tenants*

The undertenants of post-medieval Ince are not as easily divided into propertied status as their medieval predecessors. However, the documents of the period are innovative in that certain substantial holdings can be connected with specified hamlets within the township. Although the Carrhouses were referred to in 1402, it was after 1500 that this settlement, together with Lady Green and Northend, appeared as distinctive areas. In a grant of 1509, Robert, son and heir of William Blundell, gave to Thomas his brother, amongst other lands, 'eight acres arable in a close called the Hee Medowe in a place called Carre Houses' (Lancs. RO DDIn 53/74). William Edwardson held the Carrhouse and associated properties from the trustees of the Blundells' forfeited estates by a lease of 1632-33. The total acreage of the Carrhouse group at this date was 16.3.05 acres which was clearly one of the larger holdings in the township. By a Molyneux rental of 1644, money was levied at 'Northend and Ince' emphasising the separateness of the areas (Lancs. RO DDM 12/31). The Molyneux and Blundell surveys of 1769 and 1770 likewise specified property at Northend and Lady

Green (Lancs. RO DDM 14/12; DDIn 63/62).

The tenants of Ince, even in the early 19th century, owed economic allegiance to the two principal landowning families, the Molyneuxes of Sefton and the Blundells of Ince. The tithe award does identify eight other landowners who, except for William Blundell, did not possess more than 10 acres each (Lancs. RO DRL 1/40). Given that the schedule for the tithe listed seventy-six dwellings, a cursory comparison with the thirty people named in the 14th century poll tax reveals at once the demographic changes between the two periods. Ironically, the growth of the township appears to have created two contradictory movements: consolidation of ownership by the larger magnates accompanied by dispersal of land amongst their tenants. Of the medieval free tenantry, only the Blanchards remained in name with Richard Blanchard holding 84.00.39 statute acres from Thomas Weld Blundell, Joseph Blanchard holding a cottage from the Earl of Sefton and Richard and widow Blanchard owning two small areas themselves. By the early 19th century, the names of the principal tenants bore no relationship, in general, to their medieval counterparts. The Grange Estate, containing at this time 298.1.24 statute acres, was held by Elizabeth Westhead from the Earl of Sefton. The landed families were apparently retreating to their capital residencies and leaving the old manorial holdings in the occupation of others.

3.2.3 *Land management*

An analysis of land management in post-medieval Ince is substantially enlightened by the range of documents. The cumbersome identification of land in the medieval vill is superseded by estate surveys and maps which establish an overview of landownership in the township. Unfortunately, an insight into the organisation of communal management in Ince is rendered largely impossible by the absence of manorial court records. Without written evidence of the workings of the adminstrative machinery, certain lines of research have to be followed through implied references contained in other material.

Throughout the period from the 16th to the 19th century, the townfields remained the focal point in the common agrarian systems. 'Townfield' was principally a generic term embracing the fields and lands of the medieval period which had been worked in an open system. In a conveyance of 1616, the property granted included a 'butt in the Townfield called Gabelands' and 'land in the Townfield called the Lower Wranglands' (Lancs. RO DDIn 53/90). The Townfield was far from being a remnant of medieval land management. As the survey of the Nearer Townfield in 1728/29 revealed, the Gabelands and Wranglands were intrinsic parts of this field system in which land was held in scattered strips with no apparent regular pattern (fig. 3). Attention has been drawn to the size of the townfield being relatively small in comparison with midland counterparts (Shaw 1963, 27). In historical terms, the survey of 1728/29 indicates a field in a moment of transition. It was surrounded by enclosed lands and, within its bounds, the strips (fifty in all) were held by fourteen different tenants. The largest single block of land was just over 3 roods. The potential for consolidation can be recognised when a tenant such as Jane Brown was seen to be in possession of eight separate strips. From the information afforded by the 1769 Molyneux and 1770 Blundell surveys (Lancs. RO DDM 14/12; DDIn 63/62) the evolution of the Nearer Townfield can be traced through to the tithe award of 1844 (Lancs. RO DRL 1/40). By this time the townfield was made up of nine fields and held by six tenants. Clearly it was seen by the 19th century to be more profitable to consolidate and enclose rather than maintain common arable (fig. 4).

There is evidence, however scanty, that this was not the only townfield which survived beyond 1500. A grant made in 1509 by Robert to Thomas Blundell included '½ an acre in a close called Towne Field in a place called More Shote' (Lancs. RO DDIn 53/74). Moreover, in an early 18th century lease, Richard Blundell of the Carrside gave to James Morecroft 'the pikes situate and lying in the further Common Townfield' (Lancs. RO DDIn 54/15). This reference is interesting in that it does presume a distinction between the Nearer and Further

Townfield. A pike is essentially a triangular piece of land and, in the particular case of Ince Blundell, it would appear logical to equate the pikes with Pike Hey. However, the former land was assigned to a different townfield and raises the problem of identification. From material contained in a Bargain and Sale of 1652-53 (Lancs. RO DDIn 69/14) and the Blundell 18th century leases (Lancs. RO DDIn 53), it can be seen that the terminology of the open fields is not confined to the Nearer Townfield. In a lease of 1757, the land included 'one parcell lying in the Townfield in a place called the Gooselands' (Lancs. RO DDIn 54/38). The 17th century document cites, amongst many examples, 'the headlands in the Tofts...the Butt in the Peasland...the Butts in the Old Field...Butts in the short Moore Shutt'. This was all specified as arable land and, given that the derivation of the term 'butt' emphasises the irregularity of field systems, the townfields of Ince are probably not to be found in a regulated strip system. Indeed, the distribution of land in regular acreages may have been a post-medieval phenomenen. 'A note of every man's dyke lying in the Newfield Copps' compiled in 1604 indicated division into quarters *viz* Ince quarter, Altker quarter, Morehouse quarter and Northend quarter (Lancs. RO DDBl 54/3). The document is most interesting for its revelation of land division. Every quarter was divided into doles each of which contained eleven acres, more or less. The acres were distributed in varying proportions amongst the tenants and the apportionment of land to each person was clearly pre-determined and regular. This was reiterated in documents which cover the 17th and 18th centuries (Lancs. RO DDBl 44/17-26). They were concerned with exchanges of land in the Newfield at Ince Blundell and, with only one exception, all the parcels were of two acres. The problem of equating the acreage sizes prompts caution when associating the Newfield Copps with the Newfield. It seems likely that they were one and the same and can be identified in 1844 lying to the north of the Alt Grange estate (Lancs. RO DRL 1/40).

3.2.4 *Enclosure and Emparkment*

The evidence of expansion and piecemeal enclosure in post-medieval Ince is wide-spread. In the field names such as Riddings Moss and the juxtaposition of New Moss and Old Moss, the suggestion of clearance and movement towards the margin of the township is clear. Moreover, despite the continuing documentary insight into the maintenance of open field farming in the post-medieval period, a corresponding development was the increasing frequency of enclosure. In a document of 1511/1512, the feofees of Robert Blundell gave to William his son a 'close there called the Intake late in the tenure of Thomas Syngleton' (Lancs. RO DDIn 53/77). An Intake has been defined as 'a piece of land which has been enclosed, generally from a moor, but also from a common or waterway' (Richardson 1974, 16). This may be the Intake identified on the 1844 tithe map but, more importantly, it emphasises the progression of enclosures from the medieval period.

This systematisation of a general historical trend was not confined to the leased holdings of the tenantry of Ince Blundell. The creation of the 'New Plantations' and the extension of the park around Ince Hall in the 18th century undoubtedly altered the topographical face of Ince and perhaps distracted, artificially, from examination of the expansion of the vill to the Northend. The existence of the Big Common Croft and the Little Common Croft within the park in the 19th century implies the remnants of a common system. In 1652/53 the Common Crofte had been 'lately' divided into three parts, containing both arable and pasture land, and at that time was part of the demesne holding (Lancs. RO DDIn 69/14). Its position in a more ancient common organisation was reiterated in a plan of the fields around the Old Park before enclosure c.1770 (Lancs. RO DDIn 1962, acc. no. 1653). This plan revealed that in enlarging the park boundaries, parts of the earlier fields were encompassed by the new walls. In addition, it has been suggested that the White Field (Lancs. RO DDIn 69/14) was to be found in the old park as was the site for a windmill (the names Mill Hey and Mill House Clump imply the presence of a mill, probably located at the highest point in the township). Given the medieval references to fields like the Peaslands and rights of milling, it is possible that the park, as it is represented on the 19th century tithe map, conceals the demesne land of the earlier period or another area of common fields.

Figure 4 Townfields of Ince Blundell c.1770 and 1844

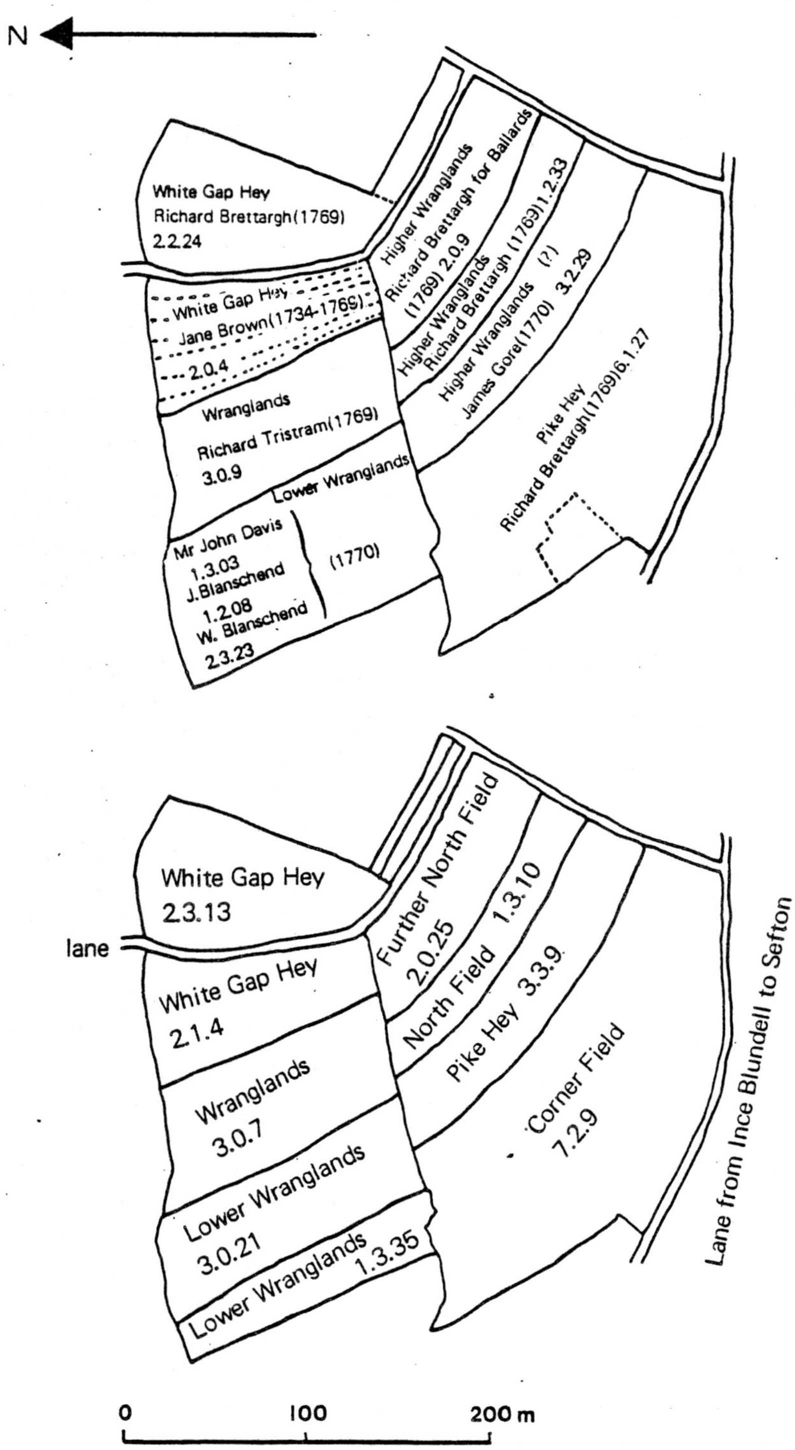

By the mid-18th century, leases and other documents concerned with the land were almost exclusively expressed in the terminology of 'closes' and 'closures'. Despite the lack of a statutory act of enclosure for Ince Blundell, it is clear that the process was affected reasonably peacefully and voluntarily. Moreover, an attempt was made to consolidate land, presumably with enclosure as an ultimate goal.

By the time of the tithe assessment of 1844, effective ownership of land in Ince Blundell lay with ten landowners, but the holdings of the Earl of Sefton and Thomas Weld Blundell far exceeded those of the others. Of the 2,075 acres of land subject to tithe payment in the township, 793 acres constituted arable as against 1,162 acres pasture or meadow. Although the preponderance of pasture over arable land may have been a post-medieval development, the reasons for this composition in the farming are not clear: it may either have been due to the need to feed local industrialised communities or merely that the nature of the marginal land at Ince was unsuitable for arable farming. Of the lands attached to Ince Blundell Hall in 1652/53, 132.0.29 customary acres were designated pasture and meadow and 93.0.17 customary acres were specified as arable indicating as early as the 17th century the predominance of pasture over arable.

Ince Blundell is indeed somewhat enigmatic. The remnants of a typical medieval village appear to exist and yet are contradicted both by the relationships and the practices of the landownership. In this context it is worth recalling the apparent assimilation of Anglo-Saxon practices and modes of expression after 1066. Ince Blundell may have represented a settlement upon which a feudal administration was developed rather than imposed. Like the bilateral manor, feudal society too was a historical abstraction. The reality of the situation in Ince may have been the ascendency of the Blundell family as informed leaders of a community whose roots ran a lot deeper. Evidently further documentary and archaeological work is required to substantiate some of the theories proposed in assessing the township's development.

4.0 **Sefton** (figs. 1 & 5)

4.1 Medieval

Perhaps the most oft quoted description of Sefton Township is that made by Thomas Pennant in 1773 'placed on a vast range of fine meadows that reach almost to the sea and in a great measure supply Liverpool with hay. It is watered by the Alt, a small trout stream; but after the first winter flood is covered with water the whole season, by reason of want of fall to carry it way' (1801, 27). As a contemporary observation of the vill, this was probably an accurate characterisation. The threat of flooding was a constant factor which undoubtedly shaped medieval and post-medieval Sefton. As the Victoria County History relates, the geology of the area was made up of the lower keuper sandstone of the new red sandstone overlaid by sand and thick boulder clay and by alluvial deposit between the village and the Alt. 'The soil varies: the subsoil is sand and clay. Wheat, barley, oats and rye are grown as well as potatoes, but cabbages are now the chief crop' (VCH 3, 1907, 66).

4.1.1 *Landowners*

According to Domesday, Sefton was held by five thegns at the death of Edward the Confessor and was assessed at one hide and was worth sixteen shillings beyond the customary rent (VCH 3, 1907, 67). As with Ince Blundell, there is no reason to suppose that the five holdings corresponded to five 'demesnes' within the township. Moreover, it is extremely difficult to equate the site of Sefton Old Hall, the Edge and the hamlets of Sefton Town, Buckley Hill and Windles Green, with the five ancient settlements. At Domesday, Sefton appears to have included the hamlets of Lunt and Netherton. However, what is certain is that in terms of overlordship, the Molyneux family of Sefton were pre-eminent throughout the period examined. In 1212, it was recorded that '*Ricardus de Mulinas tenet x Carucatas terre et dimideam de dono Rogeri Pictaviensis per servicium dimidii feodi j. militis*' (Book of Fees 1921, 208). (Richard de Mulinas holds ten carucates of land and a half of the gift of

Figure 5 Sefton: Settlement and Geology

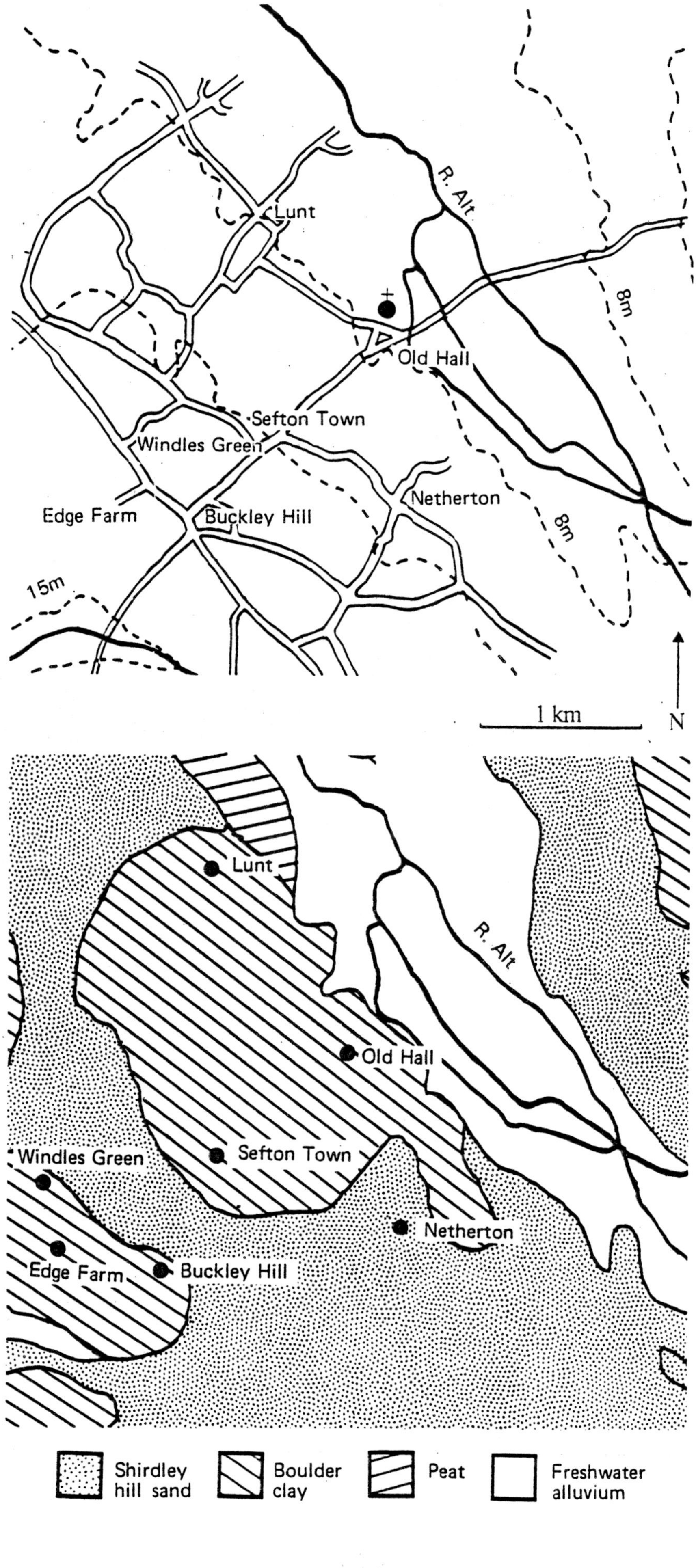

Roger the Poitevan [to his ancestor] by the service of half the fee of one knight (Farrer ed. 1903, 12). It has been suggested that the 10½ carucates were made up of the manor of Sefton and its hamlets, a third part of Thornton and a moiety of Toxteth all in the hundred of West Derby, and Cuerden in the hundred of Leyland. Whether this holding represents that with which the 'Roger' of Domesday was enfeoffed by Roger, the Poitevan has not been substantiated: he may have been the predecessor of Molyneux and not a lineal ancestor. Nevertheless, by 1212 the Molyneux family was evidently in possession of a sizeable manorial holding with other extraneous property. The 1212 Inquest also recorded that Richard Molyneux gave to Richard Branche and to Robert half a carucate in Lunt (Farrer ed. 1903, 13). Although Lunt was yet to be established as a separate entity, it was seemingly recognised as part of an estate. Richard Molyneux had also granted three bovates of land to his son, Robert (Farrer ed. 1903, 13). It seems that this land was in Netherton and constituted the parcel there known as Arland (VCH 3, 1907, 75).

Throughout the medieval period the Molyneux family held Sefton as their principal demesne and made extensive grants in the township. In a pre-1320 grant, Richard of Molineux was referred to as 'Lord of Cefton' (Lancs. RO DDM 46/11) and frequent mention was made of the Molyneuxes granting land as their demesne. In the early 13th century it would appear that Adam de Molyneux was a man of prominent status. In 1228 he was one of those commissioned to decide what parts of the forest in Lancashire should be disforested (VCH 3, 1907, 67 n10). Similarly, in 1446 Henry VI granted to Sir Richard Molyneux and his heirs the offices of master forester of the forest and parks of West Derbyshire, steward of the wapentake of Salfordshire and constable of the Castle of Liverpool (VCH 3, 1907, 69). Although the extent of Molyneux land in Sefton can be determined, it is not possible to identify the demesne with any certainty. Richard Molyneux, who died on the 6th April, 1363, held the manor of Sefton valued at about £55 of which £20 related to the rents of tenants at will. The estimated worth of the capital messuage with its appurtenances was 140 acres of arable at 2s. 0d. an acre and 80 acres of meadow at 5s. 0d. an acre (VCH 3, 1907, 68 n9).

Unlike Ince Blundell, Sefton was clearly dominated by one demesne Lord. Paradoxically, this increases the difficulty of assessing medieval subtenancies and ownership. Besides land grants, the two available documents researched which give any indication of other landholders are the Exchequer Lay Subsidy Roll for 1332 and the 14th century Poll Tax. The Lay Subsidy entry for Sefton listed ten people, one of whom Robert, the son of Richard, paid a greater levy than William de Molyneux. The list also included Robert del Ridynge who contributed the same amount as Molyneux (Rylands ed. 1896, 21). The Poll Tax levies of 1377-1381 registered forty-eight payments of 1s. 0d. from the vill of Sefton which presumably included Lunt and Netherton (PRO E1179/130/29). The reliability of the Poll Tax has already been mentioned. Robert del Ridynge (sometimes Robert of the Ruyding) was witness to a number of grants and in one of these was referred to as Robert of the Ruddying of Sefton (Lancs. RO DDM 46/22). Despite his obvious importance in the vill there is no evidence, direct or otherwise, of his actual holding. Like a number of residents associated with the township, such as Roger of the Lunde and Adam of the Gorsthil, Robert del Ridynge may also be associated with a particular area of the township. Whether this implies identification with specific estates or hamlets is not clear. It can be tentatively proposed that since 'Ridding' carries the meaning of clearance of land, Robert del Ridynge may have possessed land which was identified as being on the margin of the township.

What is certain is that the estate of the Edge was held in some eminence both in terms of land and position. In one charter, the Edge was apparently referred to as a manor (VCH 3, 1907, 72). An estate here was granted to Thomas de Molyneux by his father Richard in 1315. By the late 14th century, the estate had devolved upon Thomas the Molyneux of Keverdale as a 'place of land in Sefton called the Egge' (Lancs. RO DDM 46/43). In 1387/88 a letter of attorney certified the transfer of the Edge to Joan, the widow of Thomas (Lancs. RO

DDM 46/45). In the 15th century the Edge descended through the Osbaldestons of Osbaldeston. In a settlement dated 1461, Geoffrey Osbaldeston gave to John his son and Elizabeth his wife '...a messuage called the Egge in Sefton' (Lancs. RO DDM 46/57). In the 16th century the property reverted to the Molyneux family.

4.1.2 *Settlement*

As has been noted, the Molyneux rights in medieval Sefton were seemingly absolute. However, the absence of a village centre raises problems both in terms of land management and the relationship of the manor to the vill. There is no obvious village settlement and, indeed, no remnants of a nucleated settlement in close proximity to the old manor site. A document of 1411 supplied a 'view of decayed housing' in the Sefton area (Lancs. RO DDM 7/addl. acc. 3300). Although the document is in a severe condition of disrepair, its most interesting feature is that it may indicate long-term decay of messuages perhaps in a settlement closer to the old manorial buildings. Dispute over the status of the manor itself and the removal to Croxteth of the Molyneux family has not been resolved and the dates of the final movement vary from the 15th to the 18th centuries. In 1535, Leland recorded that 'Mr. Molyneux a knight of great lands, two miles from Prescot, dwelleth at a place called Croxteth' (VCH 3, 1907, 70). However, later documents do suggest that facilities to maintain hospitality at the manor of Sefton did remain and that possibly only its status as the capital messuage altered.

4.1.3 *Land management*

An assessment of land management is difficult owing to the paucity of evidence for the medieval period. The documentary information concerning town and common fields is virtually non-existent. In a pre-14th century grant, Robert, son of Roger of the Lunde, gave to Agnes his sister 'a house and selion adjoining, lying between the land of Robert Branche and of Richard Branche' (Lancs. RO DDM 46/8). Similarly, in a grant of 1317/18, Simon, son of Adam of the Lond, gave to Robert his son 'a place of land in the Lond...with one head abutting on the curtilage of Richard the Calverknave' and in the 13th century, Robert, son of Robert Branche of the Lund, quitclaimed to Richard Molyneux of Sefton 'a bovate of land in the Lund' (Lancs. RO DDM 46/16 and DDM 46/12 respectively). At this juncture, the presence of a common arable system can only be inferred from the above and in various field names such as Witefelt, Lond Lone, Havedland. Moreover, there is evidence that holding in severalty may have been widespread and that within this strip holdings were a feature.

A striking characteristic of the medieval land grants is the identification of holdings by their relationship to dikes and ditches. For example, in an undated document of pre-1300, William of Molineux granted to William, son of Simon of Grayne, 'that part of his demesne on the Gorstihul by these bounds, beginning at the corner in the East, and so following the dike to the corner in the West, and so following the dike to the corner in the north part and so following the dike to the said corner in the East' (Lancs. RO DDM 46/2). Likewise, in a grant made before 1289, William Molineux gave to Richard Fox '3 acres in Sefton lying below his field and Snotirsarpel as divided by dykes' (Lancs. RO DDM 46/10). The prevalence of dikes may denote two things: either the need to protect land from flooding of the River Alt or the desire to cultivate a proportion of land by enclosure. Of course, the two elements are not mutually exclusive. The need and desire to enclose and, therefore, the system of land management, may have been the direct outcome of the particular physical conditions encountered. This may itself have militated against a nucleated settlement around the Old Hall with associated classic medieval features and open fields and account for the impression of scattered hamlets. Perhaps the interpretation of the dikes in Sefton can be partly resolved by reference to an exchange of 1431 between Sir Richard Molyneux and Robert of the Ridynge. Sir Richard Molyneux received 'the mill dam made by Robert of the Rydying, on his land and his land by these bounds beginning at the mill-dam to the south opposite the end of the new dike, and so to a small oak standing in the dike of Arland, then following that dike as far as the said mill-dam, and so following that dam to the first bound' (Lancs. RO DDM 46/51). In this context it would appear that the dikes were used specifically to protect the land from the Alt. As an interesting aside, if the Arland stated in the document is equatable with the Little Ireland, Old Ireland and Barley Ireland of the 1769 Molyneux Survey, it seems that Robert of Rydyinges' estate was probably centred upon Netherton (Lancs. RO DDM 14/47). As a hamlet, Netherton does not seem to be viewed as a separate entity until the 17th century.

One area of the township which can be identified from medieval sources is the Pepperfield. It lay in the west of the manor at Lunt (Lancs. RO DDM 14/47). In a pre-1213 grant, Richard of Mulinas gave to Simon his brother '6 selions on the culture of Sefton at Thorinton, extending in width from Pepirfelt to the next way from Crossbi to the church' (Lancs. RO DDM 46/1). Likewise, in 1294, the Pepperfield in Sefton, was made up of 6 acres of land lying near to the Hanecroft, and was given by Richard de Molyneux to his son Peter (VCH 3, 1907, 72). A number of grants were thenceforth recorded in the medieval period culminating in Henry Blundell giving to Robert, son of John Molyneux of Melling in 1454-5, a pound of pepper with the field called Pepperfield. Such observations excepted, it is difficult to trace any basic trends or influences without further definite evidence of medieval landownership. Ironically, it is the post-medieval documentation in which remnants of medieval land use may be discerned, which throws greater light upon the earlier epoch.

4.2 Post-medieval

4.2.1 *Settlement* (figs. 5 & 6)

The most obvious feature of Sefton in its later phase is the definition of the township in terms of separate hamlets. Netherton and Lunt became identified as individual townships although the realities of landownership did not conform to the artificial boundaries. As the 1845 tithe schedule reveals, the township was virtually under the sole ownership of the Earl of Sefton (Lancs. RO DRL 1/72). Any other holdings not in lease from the Sefton estates were, in the main, small cottages, crofts and gardens. The impressions of the pattern of overlordship in the medieval period are thus confirmed (Lancs. RO DDM 14/12). However, it is also clear that the principal demesne had removed to Croxteth. By the early 17th century, the Molyneux estates had reached their greatest extent and showed the widespread characteristic of extrinsic holdings (VCH 3, 1907, 70). Moreover, the family's social and political status reflected the importance of this regional land base. Richard, Viscount Molyneux of Maryborough, died in 1636 at Croxteth in possession of the hereditary offices of forester of West Derbyshire etc... In terms of land, he was also said to be holding, amongst other properties, the manors of Sefton, Netherton and Lunt; the five 'ploughlands' being the twelfth part of a knight's fee (VCH 3, 1907, 70 n22).

Despite the prominence of the Molyneuxes, documents of post-1500 date give a greater insight into the subtenantry of Sefton township. A rental of William Molyneux for 1515 listed the names of families which were common throughout the period (Lancs. RO DDM 12/27). The rental cited eighteen people in total holding from the Molyneuxes and, although it is difficult to discern any standardisation in the amounts levied, the wife of Jacob Lunt, John Derwyn and Hugh Ashton all contribute the highest rate of 8s. 11d. In an earlier rental of 1509, the list for Sefton again included eighteen contributors, the majority of whom correspond with those paying six years later (Lancs. RO DDM 12/26) (Appendix 2). This particular rental is more interesting in two respects. Firstly, it associated particular individuals with specified fields and, secondly, it names the freeholders who presumably fell under the manorial legislation of the Sefton demesne. John Molyneux paid 6d. for Arland and the 'successors of Osbalston' paid 1d. for 'le Egge' and made a contribution of 12d. for 'le Gorstefild'. The repeated appearance of these areas in earlier documents for the medieval period suggests that their freehold status may perhaps have existed at the time of the Domesday Survey or be of even earlier origin. The history of the settlement of the Edge to

Figure 6 Sefton 1769

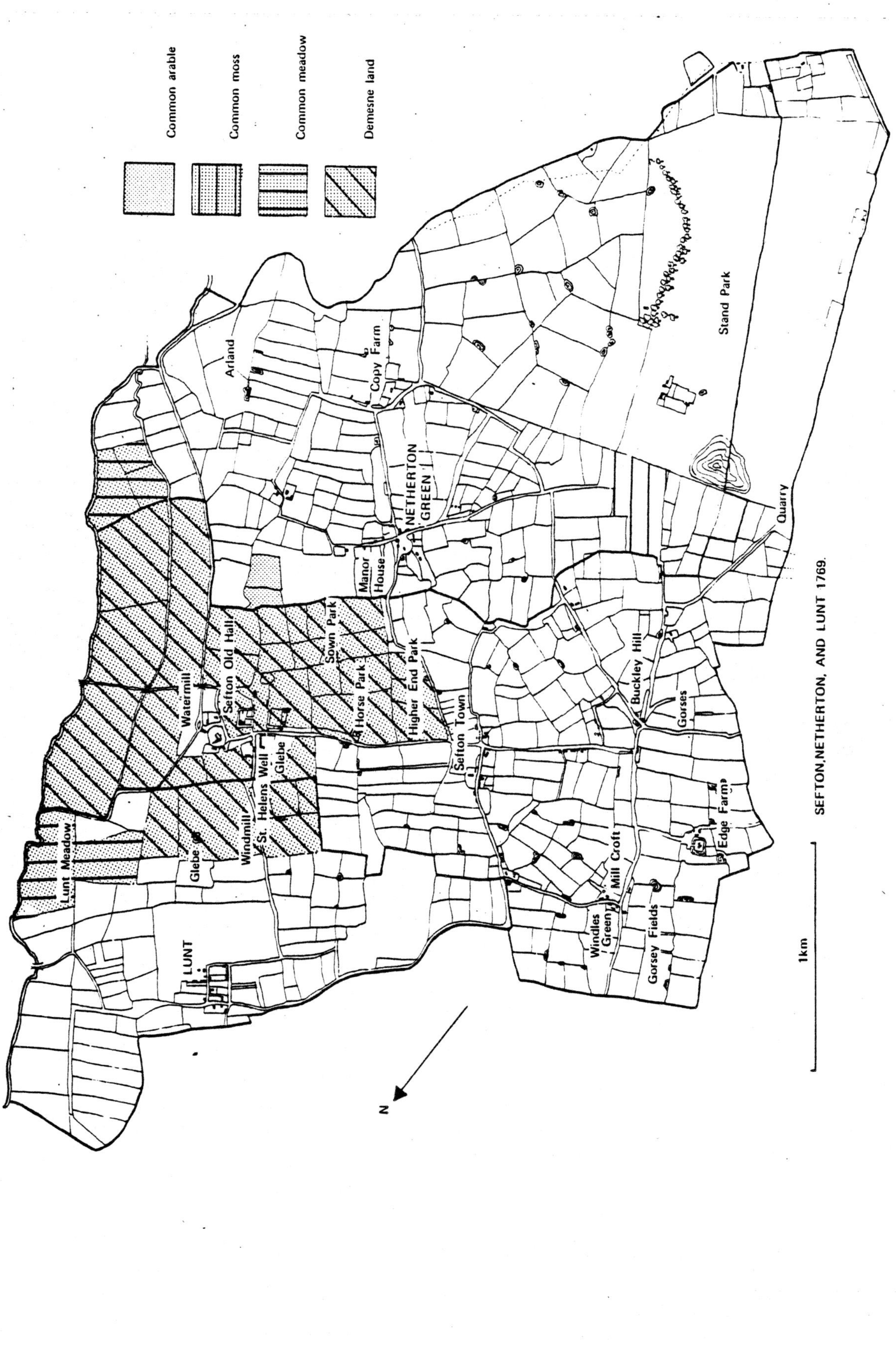

this juncture has been discussed. On its reversion to the Molyneuxes, the Edge devolved upon the Baron family in the 17th century, Lawrence Baron petitioning in 1652 for the restoration to him of a part of the tenement, two thirds of his grandfather's estate having previously been sequestered for recusancy (VCH 3, 1907, 74). At Lady Day in 1664, Lawrence Buron (*sic*) was assessed at five hearths (PRO E/179/250/11). In 1666 Lawrence Baron and Alice his mother, paid for six hearths (VCH 3, 1907, 74 n3). Until the 18th century the Edge was held by the Barons; in 1790 Thomas Ormisher was the occupant (Lancs. RO DDM 46/220) and at the time of the tithe assessment it was held by James Birch (Lancs. RO DRL 1/72). Given that the holding at the Edge was associated with a moat, the documentary and archaeological suggestions combine to indicate a site of some importance.

The establishment and colonisation of the hamlets of Sefton Town, Windles Green and Buckley Hill is endowed with no such illuminating chronology. It is possible that the clusters of dwellings at these sites were in part determined by the junction of carriageways and routes within the township and there is no clear documentary evidence to imply that they had developed from medieval settlements. An assessment of the topographical and geological evidence is of no more assistance in locating settlement in the township as a whole. The known medieval sites at Sefton Old Hall, Lunt and Netherton all lie at an uncomfortably low altitude in view of the problems of flooding from the River Alt. An examination of the distribution of soils at these sites shows that all are situated in areas of imperfect or poor drainage. In contrast, Sefton Town, Windles Green and Buckley Hill are a little more elevated and may have been more attractive for settlement for topographical reasons. As elsewhere, the drainage properties of the soils are imperfect or poor, and it is only at Sefton Town that early settlement might be more confidently predicted. In general, it seems that the problems of identification of settlement in these areas might be answered only by recourse to archaeological methods of landscape survey and investigation.

4.2.2 *Land management*

The documentary material available for detailing land management in the post-1500 era is, however, more fruitful. Manorial court rolls for Sefton are extant for the 18th and 19th centuries. They listed both freeholders and leaseholders for Sefton, Lunt and Netherton, in addition to noting the appointments of officers such as Lookers to Cops and Goats and Barley Men and judgements principally concerned with communal conventions, such as the upkeep of ditches and the rights of inheritance (Lancs. RO DDM 7/278 and 280). Although these were essentially institutions which had become virtually moribund by the late 18th century, they are valuable in the context of this assessment for two major reasons: they indicate the differentiations in terms of tenurial contracts and, at the same time, stress that the administration of the township demanded certain communal activities. Whether the system was created by the manorial lord or had sprung from within the community is largely irrelevant. What is important is the emphasis upon common practices and their control within the demesne administration. As an entry for 1785 records, 'We the Juryors of this court do find all such Persons who have not open Platts in the said lowlands where needful to lay and open suffisheath between and 1st of Augst next or we lay each Platt 5s.' (Lancs. RO DDM 7/278). The example cited underlines the requirement of people to open up their lowland holdings, presumably for common grazing, at a specified time of the year. The notion of common land for pasture, under the ownership of the lord, seems to imply some arrangement for common arable farming. However, the topographical evidence for this is not immediately obvious.

In the 1845 tithe schedule the references to communal agriculture were, in the main, concerned with pasture and meadow (Lancs. RO DRL 1/72). Moreover, the expanses of lowland meadow which run alongside the River Alt in proximity to the old manorial settlement were often referred to as 'old' meadow and 'old' pasture, clearly delineating them from modern expansion and farming practices. In relating this information to arable farming the Molyneux survey of 1769 contained a number of field names which presumably may have represented earlier common systems (e.g. Sefton Field, Great Field, Rushy Butts) (Lancs. RO DDM 14/12). However, by the post-medieval period, no land in Sefton was divided into strips along the lines of the Ince Blundell townfield. This may seem surprising given the predominance of arable farming over pasture in this particular township. For the tithe of 1845, just over 952 acres of titheable land was designated as arable as against a little more than 176 acres of meadow or pasture (Lancs. RO DRL 1/72). This begs the question as to how land use in the township was determined by, or indeed determined, the relationship between the demesne and the village.

As has been noted, settlement and organisation must have been intimately linked to the tendency of the River Alt to flood. The Sefton Meadows were marked on the six inch Ordnance Survey map of 1850 (sheet 99) as 'Subject to Floods'. In a letter written by Joseph Thomson, rector of Sefton in 1648, the problems were not underestimated: 'I made soe many motions about the River Alt that for some reasons I grow wearie...many of our neighbours are driven out of their ground by water...and have neither meadow ground nor pasture for their cattle' (Lancs. RO QSP 3/10). Such observations underline the probable importance of strict manorial control over the farming practices on the pasture and meadow land. The documentary evidence reveals many aspects of land organisation in this context. An account of Sefton demesnes for 1654 itemised the division of the Milne Meadow, Oversbridge, The Litle Carr, The Sowen Carr and the Great Carr into regular 'doles' amongst the undertenantry in return for standardised rental payments (Lancs. RO DDM 1/46). Areas within each meadow were reserved for 'house use' and were presumably worked by direct management methods. 'A Catalogue of ye Hay Gotten for my Lords Use att Sephton in ye yeare 1687' is illuminating in that it records the amounts of hay made by the individual tenants and also wage payments made for mowing in the different meadows of the town (Lancs. RO DDM 11/25). The payment of money wages for labour implies the getting of hay for commercial purposes and probably supports the notion of the growing of the crop for use in Liverpool. The accounts contained numerous references to work done in the meadows and pastures. For example, in accounts for July 1654, one item recorded 'paid unto John Wignall and Nic. Carlton for ditchinge and Hedgeinge att harbridge and betweene the Medowes and pasture ground and for Cuttinge Wood and Carryinge the same tow hedge either ten dayes/att seaven the day = 11s. 8d.' (Lancs. RO DDM 1/62). Such work was obviously of prime importance to prevent cattle straying on to meadowland and crops. More particularly, ditching was presumably essential in the low areas to facilitate drainage. The manorial court rolls often listed amercements for the non-scouring of ditches between different holdings. Ultimately, ditching and hedging may be the superficial evidence of the long-term movement towards enclosure. The vast majority of leases granted in the late 17th and early 18th centuries included the right to enclose acreages on Sefton Moss (Lancs. RO DDM 46). One section of the calendar series deals exclusively with acres granted 'lying at the corner of the park wall' (Lancs. RO DDM 46/96-104).

The division and enclosure of the moss instigated by the lord of the manor is a prime example of the continuing influence of the Molyneux family. Despite the move to Croxteth, intricate accounts were kept of the upkeep of the Sefton demesne and its farming. Permission was granted for enclosure from the waste and may indicate the recognition of the advantages this preferred for the increase in agricultural productivity. Remnants of the obligations of the feudal society also remained. A document from the late 17th century outlined rent hens due at Michaelmas: fifteen from Sefton, ten from Netherton and eight from Lunt (Lancs. RO DDM 11/40). Likewise a lease of 1754 from Thomas Molyneux to John Darwin of Sefton demanded service including the plowing of one roodland of ground in Sefton demesne, making a roodland of grass into hay, carting a load of turf to Sefton Hall and corn to be ground at the mill of Thomas Molyneux in Sefton.

Clearly, despite the apparent lack of a nucleated settlement around the manorial site, the land administration of vill and demesne was closely intertwined. The difficulty of tracing a medieval open field system does not necessarily mean that holding in severalty was dominant in the medieval period. On the contrary, the presence of a strong overlordship tends to deflect evidence from the vill to the working of the demesne and makes an historical assessment of land use difficult.

5.0 Comments

The examination of landownership in Ince Blundell and Sefton was intended to develop a number of lines for further investigation. Any conclusions can only be as definitive as the evidence upon which they are based. The contrast in land ownership and tenure between the townships is clearly expressed in the documentation. Its interpretation in terms of the landscape and settlement patterns is less easily understood. On the one hand the manorial administration of Sefton indicates a pattern of tenure and land management recognised in other areas of England, but it has been pointed out that the effect of a strong overlordship in Sefton appears to have resulted in a lack of positive evidence regarding the identification of settlement and land-use. However, it is likely that more intensive detailed work in tracing the documentary history of known sites in the 18th and 19th centuries may be possible through an assessment of leases and rentals at least for the post-medieval period. In contrast, Ince Blundell still retains many of the physical elements of manor, village and open field agriculture, but expresses none of the usual manorial administration. A closer examination of the relationship between the Barony and the landowners and their tenants in Ince Blundell is essential, both in documentary and archaeological terms.

As has been suggested, the study was viewed as a basis for investigation into tenurial relationships in general. In both Ince Blundell and Sefton it was felt that a greater insight was required into the activities and status of the subtenantry. If this could be achieved, more light might be thrown not only upon the manorial structure but upon the status of known archaeological sites. This in turn is of value in identifying those sites which are likely to provide archaeological information and can be used in assessing priorities for detailed fieldwork or excavation. In addition, documentary research of the detailed nature described above may also result in the identification of estate and property boundaries and in turn by imposing these on to the modern landscape lead to recognition in the field of hitherto unknown sites.

Abbreviations:

Chet Soc	Chetham Society
Lancs. RO	Lancashire Record Office, Preston
PRO	Public Record Office, London
Rec Soc	Record Society of Lancashire and Cheshire
THSLC	Transactions of the Historic Society of Lancashire and Cheshire
VCH	Victoria County History

6.0 References and Select Bibliography

Anderson, P. 1974 *Passages from Antiquity to Feudalism,* London

Book of Fees 1921 *Liber Feodorum: the Book of Fees commonly called Testa de Nevill* I AD 1198-1242, London

Campbell, B. 1981 'Commonfield Origins: The Regional Dimension' in Rowley, T. *The Origins of Open Field Agriculture* 112-129, London

Caroe, W.D. & Gordon, E.J.A. 1893 *Sefton: A Descriptive and Historical Account,* London

Dodgshon, R. 1981 'The Interpretation of sub-divided fields: a study in private or communal interests' in Rowley, T. *The Origins of Open Field Agriculture* 130-144, London

Ekwall, E. 1922 *The Place Names of Lancashire,* Manchester

Elliot, G. 1973 'Field Systems of Northwest England' in Baker, A. & Butlin, R. *Studies of Field Systems in the British Isles* 42-92, London

Farrer, W. (ed) 1903 'Lancashire Inquests, Extents and Feudal Aids 1 1205-1307' *Rec Soc* 48 (for 1903-04)

Gibson, T.E. 1876 *Lydiate Hall and its Associations,* Edinburgh

Hoskins, W.G. 1955 *The Making of the English Landscape,* Harmondsworth

Morton, T.N. 1881 'Ince Blundell Charters' *THSLC* 33 (for 1880-81) 265-67

Morton, T.N. 1883 'Ancient Deeds' *THSLC* 34 (for 1881-82) 135-41

Morton, T.N. 1928 Blundell Deeds at Ince Blundell Hall, unpublished, Liv. RO Hq 333.33(72)MOR

Morton, T.N. & Gibson, T.E. 1880 'Ancient Charters, Ince Blundell Collection' *THSLC* 32 (for 1879-80) 194-96

Pennant, T. 1801 *A Tour from Downing to Alston Moor 1773,* London

Postan, M.M. 1972 *The Medieval Economy and Society,* London

Richardson, J. 1974 *The Local Historian's Encyclopedia,* New Barnet

Rowley, T. (ed) 1981 *The Origins of Open Field Agriculture,* London

Rylands, J.P. (ed) 1896 'The Exchequer Lay Subsidy Roll 1332' Miscellanies Lancs. and Ches. 2 *Rec Soc* 31 (for 1894-95) 1-28

Shaw, R.C. 1963 'The Townfields of Lancashire' *THSLC* 114 (for 1962) 23-26

Singleton, J.F. 1964 'The Influence of Geographical Factors on the Common Fields of Lancashire'*THSLC* 115 (for 1963) 31-40

Taylor, C.C. 1981 'Archaeology and the Origins of Open-field Agriculture' in Rowley, T. *The Origins of Open Field Agriculture* 13-21, London

Tyrer, F. 1963 'The Common Fields of Little Crosby' *THSLC* 114 (for 1962) 37-48

VCH 1907 *Victoria History of the Counties of England: A History of the County of Lancashire* 3, London

Vinogradoff, P. 1892 *Villeinage in England,* Oxford

Wainwright, F.T. 1975 *Scandinavian England* Finberg, H.P. (ed), Chichester

Walker, F. 1939 'Historical Geography of South West Lancashire before the Industrial Revolution' *Chet Soc* ns 103

Wilson, G.S. 1980 'The Land Tax and West Derby Hundred 1780-1831' *THSLC* 129 (for 1979) 63-92

Youd, G. 1962 'The Common Fields of Lancashire' *THSLC* 113 (for 1961) 1-43

7.0 Appendices

7.1 Grant of land in Ince Blundell in 1402 (Lancs. RO DDIn 53/55)

Grant: John of the Wodes, chaplain, John of Becaneshowe and Henry Dobbesone to John Blundell of Ines...all properties in the Carhouses in Carhousehey, except Messuages held by William of the Holt and Allice Coppok, and a garden called the Foxeyord;

also

3 selions on the Grayndelondez,
1 selion abutting on the Grenehull,
1 selion in the Meelegates,
1 selion on the Holdefeld,
2 selions on the Grangelondez which abutt towards the field of Richard Blanchard,
3 selions on the Peyselondez,
1 selion on the Rayrakres,
2 selions on the Carcold,
1 selion on the Hokengreves which Ellen Blanchard holds,
1 selion on the Reyselonds Pitt in the Goselond on the Peyselondes,
2 selions which lie between the Peyselondez in the Mylnehill,
2 selions on the Rayracres,
headland upon the Toftelondes,
1 selion upon the Selacres,
1 selion called the H...londs Waynyng,
1 headland upon the Hokengreves,
1 place of land called the Marledhey next the Peyselondes which William Dobbesone and Henry the Taylliour hold,
5 selions on the Faregreves,
4 selions upon the Quytefeld,
3 selions upon the Carcold,
3 selions upon the Fernylondes,
3 selions upon the Scholebrodes,
1 selion on the Peyselondes which William Foxe holds,
1 selion lying between the Peyselondes & the Toftelondez,
2 selions on the Meelegates,
1 selion on the Wrangelondez which abutt on the field of Richard Blanchard,
1 selion on the Holdfeld which Alan son of Roger holds,
8 ac. meadow called the Heymedo,
service and rent of Thomas Ballard 3s. 6d.,
Simon of Ines 21d.,
Thomas Ballard and Joan widow of Thomas the Molyneux for properties which belonged to John of Orshagh 15d.,
Richard of Monyley 3d.,
1 messuage 2 selions in the Nethercarcold,
1 selion on the Haregreves,
3 selions on the Peyselandez,
2 selions on the Tornage called the Coltesland and the Coppokesland,
2 selions on the Sondebeckes,
4 selions on the Wallebutte which abut on the Dowlache,
2 selions which abut on the garden of John Cook,
1 selion on the Gapelondez which John Cook holds,
1 messuage 5 crofts and 2 selions on the Gapelondes which Mary widow of Adam son of William holds,
1 messuage 3 selions on the Ouyterfield,
2 selions on the Fernylondes,
2 selions next the Mylnehill,
1 selion on the Tottelondez,
3 selions on the Cellacres,

2 selions on the Tatetez which abut towards the Greenhull,
1 selion on the Meelgatez,
1 selion on the Holdefeld,
1 selion on the Wrangelondez which abutts towards the field of Richard Blanchard,
2 selions on the Peyselandez of which 1 abuts towards the Marledherth and one Called the Fynyll,
2 selions on the Gapelondez,
1 selion between the highway and the Meelgatez which John of Orsagh holds,
and 1 garden which Henry son of William holds,
all in Ince Blundell - to John Blundell for life, then to William son of William Blundell of Ines and Alice daughter of Nicholas Blundell and their issue.

7.2 Rental of the lands of William Molyneux 1509 (Lancs. RO DDM 12/26)

Rentalle Willi molyneux Armiga [1509]

It Jacobo lunte			viij s	xj d
It Johe Derwynd			viij s	xj d
[illegible...]			viij s	xj d
	Sm̄		xxvj s	ix d
Sefton				
It Henrico Hurder			vj s	ij d
It eodm. p̄. Snotacrr			ij s	
It eod Hen p̄. Stonebrig				xviij d
It Johe Mellyng Smyth			vij s	[erased]j d
It eodm p̄. Snotacrr				
It Willmo fferr[es]			vij s	x d
It Thoma Tyer			vij s	vj d
It eod Thoma p̄. Stonebrig				xviij d
It Thoma Hulme			vj s	viij d
It Willmo Fairclogh			vj s	vj d ob
It uxe Johe Hesketh				xij d
It Robto [Caske]		[illegible]		
It Thoma Penyngton			v s	vj d
It Johe Mellyng Jun			x s	iij d
It uxe Willo dolby			vj s	ij d ob
It Henrico parr			x s	
It Edmndo Croston			vj s	viij d
It Johe Sefton			ix s	iij d
It Margareta Buckeley			v s	iiij d
	Sm̄	v l		xij d
Netherton				
It Johe Coke			vij s	
It Thoma Irland			v s	xj d
It Robto Derwynt			v s	iiij d
It Johe Sothwrth. sen.			iij s	v d
It Henrico dale			iiij s	viij d
It Johe Hunte			vj s	
It Rogero Irland			ij s	iiij d
	Sm̄		xxxiiij s	viij d
Netherton carr				
It Johe Coke			vj s	viij d
It Thoma Irland			vj s	viij d
It Robto Derwynt			vj s	viij d
It Johe Sothwrth			vj s	viij d
It Henrico dale			vj s	viij d
It Johe hunte			vj s	viij d
It Johe hurdes			vj s	viij d
	Sm̄	ij l	vj s	viij d
le Walle milne				
It Thoma. Irland			v s	iij d
It Rico. lunte			v s	iij d
It eod Rico.			ij s	viij d
It eodm Rico.				xxj d
It Rogero Irland			iij s	vj d
It p̄sevelo Croston			ij s	viij d

It eodm			ij^{s}	viij^{d}
It Willmo. Irland			ij^{s}	viij^{d}
It uxe. Robt. Irland			ij^{s}	viij^{d}
It uxe. Thoma. Croston			ij^{s}	viij^{d}
	Sm̄		xxxj^{s}	ix^{d}
le Colts medowe				
It Johe Mellyng			vij^{s}	
Horse Hey				
It Nicho. Wetherby			x^{s}	
Sefton Medowe				
It Johe Sefton			vj^{s}	
Ibem hoke				
It Henrico. Hurdes			vij^{s}	iiij^{d}
It uxe. Thoma. Crosto.			ij^{s}	
It Nicho Wetherby			ij^{s}	
It Henrico Derwynt)				xij^{d}
p̄. le Damme Stydde)				
	Sm̄		xxxv^{s}	iiij^{d}
ffoxe medowe				
It Jacobo lunt			ij^{s}	iiij^{d}
It Johe. Derwynt			ij^{s}	iiij^{d}
It Johe Hunt			iij^{s}	vj^{d}
It Hugoe Ashton			ij^{s}	iiij^{d}
It Johe. Coke			iij^{s}	vj^{d}
	Sm̄		xiiij^{s}	
le Nuefild				
It Thoma Irland			iij^{s}	vj^{d}
It Rogero Derwynt			iij^{s}	vj^{d}
[illegible]				
It Rico [lokke]			iij^{s}	vj^{d}
	Sm̄		xiiij^{s}	
Liba firma de Sefton				
It Johe Molyneux p̄. Arland				vj^{d}
It Johe Swyfte			ij^{s}	
It Johe Hurder				xij^{d}
It Mather Male p̄. le damestid				j^{d} ob
It hered Willo Rydyng			iij^{s}	iiij^{d}
It hered Osbalston p̄. le Egge				j^{d}
It eisdm p̄. Cotag. i. Netherto				j^{d}
It eisdm p̄. le Gorstefild				xij^{d}
It Willmo. Sefton				xxiij^{d}
[illegible]				
It Johe. lunte				xix^{d} ob
It Nicho. Wetherby				xviij^{d}
It Rico [Albeke]				xiij^{d}
It Rico ffoller			iij^{s}	
It Nicho Blundell Ar.)				iiij^{d}
p̄. manio de p̄va Crosby)				
	Sm̄		xvij^{s}	xj^{d}
	Sm̄ to^{l}	xvj^{l}	ij^{s}	j^{d}

Magna Crosby			
It Johe. Derwynt		xiiij^{s}	
It Henr. Nichson		v^{s}	
It Willmo. lunt		v^{s}	
It eodm p̄...		ij^{s}	
It uxe hugo Molyneux p̄...		ij^{s}	
It Johe Robynson		iiij^{s}	
	Sm̄	xxxij^{s}	
Ince Blundell			
It Rico Wilson		vj^{s}	
Ince carr			
It Rico Wilson			xij^{d}
It Johe. Fletewode			xij^{d}
It Johe. Coke			xij^{d}
It [Blena] Blanchard			xij^{d}
It Rico. Robynson		iij^{s}	
It henr. Robynson			xij^{d}
	Sm̄	xiiij^{s}	